Charles H. Spurgeon's
Little Instruction Book

HONOR
BOOKS

Tulsa, Oklahoma

Charles H. Spurgeon's Little Instruction Book
ISBN 1-56292-159-2
Copyright © 1996 by Honor Books, Inc.
P.O. Box 55388
Tulsa, OK 74155

Compiled by James S. Bell

INTRODUCTION

Charles Haddon Spurgeon (1834-92) was an English Baptist preacher, born in Kelvedon, Essex. In 1854, at the age of 19, he became pastor of the New Park Street Chapel, London. A man who heard him preach in his first year of the pastorate made a glowing prediction:

...His name is Charles Spurgeon. He is only a boy, but he is the wonderful *preacher* in the world. He is absolutely perfect in his oratory; and, besides that, a master in the art of acting...His power was never equaled. Now, mark my words, boys, that young man will live to be the greatest preacher of this or any other age. He will bring more souls to Christ than any man who ever proclaimed the gospel, not excepting the apostle Paul. His name will be known everywhere, and his sermons will be translated into many of the languages of the world.

☞ IT PROVED TO BE A ☜ PHENOMENAL PROPHECY!

The Metropolitan Tabernacle, seating 6,000, was erected for Spurgeon in 1861. He was known as "The Prince of Preachers" and is described by many as the greatest preacher of all time.

Note: All quotes are Charles H. Spurgeon unless otherwise indicated.

HIS MOMENT OF CONVERSION

"Young man, [said the preacher] you look very miserable ...look to Jesus Christ...You have nothin' to do but to look and live." "I saw at once the way of salvation...Oh! I looked until I could almost have looked my eyes away.

"There and then the cloud was gone, the darkness had rolled away, and that moment I saw the sun; and I could have risen that instant, and sung with the most enthusiastic of them, of the precious blood of Christ, and the simple faith which looks alone to Him."

INNER SENSES AWAKEN!

"Jesus Christ is light to the eye, honey to the taste, music to the ear, joy to the heart."

—————

May the God of hope fill you with all joy and peace as you trust in him, so that you may overflow with hope by the power of the Holy Spirit.

ROMANS 15:13 NIV

JOY IN RECEIVING

"There is as much joy in the heart of God when He forgives, as there is in the heart of the sinner when he is forgiven. God is as blessed in giving as we are in receiving."

The Lord is slow to anger, abounding in love and forgiving sin and rebellion.

NUMBERS 14:18 NIV

PAID IN GOD'S TIME

"If the love of God sets us to work, the God of love will find us wages. God is a sure paymaster, though He does not always pay at the end of every week."

Be ye strong therefore, and let not your hands be weak: for your work shall be rewarded.

2 CHRONICLES 15:7

THE WEIGHT DOESN'T MATTER

"In weighty matters wait on God. And count nothing too light to be brought to the mercy seat."

Be careful for nothing; but in every thing by prayer and supplication with thanksgiving let your requests be made known unto God.

PHILIPPIANS 4:6

DID YOU KNOW?

When Spurgeon was an unconverted ten year old, a visiting missionary predicted he would preach to thousands in the largest evangelical church in London. His words came true.

THE COLD ONES DON'T COUNT

"Cold prayers are called prayers but are no prayers. They are prayers in name only."

And when thou prayest, thou shalt not be as the hypocrites are: for they love to pray standing in the synagogues and in the corners of the streets, that they may be seen.

MATTHEW 6:5

BLESSINGS IN DISGUISE

"Bless God for your afflictions,
and your afflictions will be
your greatest blessings."

***

*Consider it pure joy, my
brothers, whenever you face
trials of many kinds, because
you know that the testing of
your faith develops perseverance.*

JAMES 1:2-3 NIV

DON'T DAMPEN THE FLAME

"A Christian should be a lamp, and not a damp. He should cheer and enlighten his brethren, and never act as a wet blanket to their zeal."

Let your light shine before men, that they may see your good deeds and praise your Father in heaven.

MATTHEW 5:16 NIV

"Sincerity is the salt of the sacrifice. Without it the offering can never be acceptable to God."

SINCERELY SACRIFICIAL

By faith Abraham, when God tested him, offered Isaac as a sacrifice. He who had received the promises was about to sacrifice his one and only son.

HEBREWS 11:17 NIV

DID YOU KNOW?

Four years after his conversion, Spurgeon received the call to become the pastor of the historic New Park Street Baptist Church. He began his pastorate at nineteen years of age. He grew the largest evangelical congregation in the world.

THE FULLNESS OF HIS LOVE

"Our love to God arises out of our want: His love to us out of His fullness."

But God commendeth his love toward us, in that, while we were yet sinners, Christ died for us.

ROMANS 5:8

FAITH'S SUBLIME SIMPLICITY

"Nothing is simpler than faith, and nothing more sublime. Faith is simple from the human side: it is a childlike trust. But it is sublime from the divine side, since it grasps the Invisible, and has power with the Omnipotent."

If you have faith as small as a mustard seed...nothing will be impossible for you.

MATTHEW 17:20 NIV

DEBTORS TO THE DONOR

"Where God becomes a donor, man becomes a debtor. Every gift of grace involves a debt of gratitude."

O give thanks unto the Lord, for he is good: for his mercy endureth for ever.

PSALM 107:1

DID YOU KNOW?

By 1878, forty-eight new churches were established under
his guidance in London alone.

EXREME OPPORTUNITY

"Man's extremity is God's opportunity. When we are quite empty the Lord will fill us."

_____

My strength is made perfect in weakness.
2 CORINTHIANS 12:9

THE STAR MINISTER

"Ministers should be stars to give light, not clouds to obscure. In some cases the text is as clear as a mirror, till the preacher's breath bedims it."

———

Thy word is a lamp unto my feet, and a light unto my path.

PSALM 119:105

THE SACRED TEXT OF THE WORLD

"Newspapers are the Bibles of worldlings. How diligently they read them! Here they find their law and profits, their judges and chronicles, their epistles and revelations."

All scripture is given by inspiration of God, and is profitable for doctrine, for reproof, for correction, for instruction in righteousness.

2 TIMOTHY 3:16

A TEMPTATION FOR EVERY TASTE

"The devil entangles the youthful with beauty, the miser with gold, the ambitious with power, the learned with false doctrine. [Each] has his peculiarly adapted temptations."

———

But when you are tempted, [God] will also provide a way out so that you can stand up under it.

1 CORINTHIANS 10:13 NIV

DID YOU KNOW?

He baptized his young love and fiancé, Susannah Thompson, who later at age thirty-three, became an invalid due to illness. She began a book fund for pastors who could not afford them.

GRACE LIFTED ME

"The trials of the Christian life you shall find heavy, but...grace will make them light."

_____

My grace is sufficient for thee.
2 CORINTHIANS 12:9

A GOOD SOAK IN THE SCRIPTURES

"I would rather lay my soul asoak in half a dozen verses [of the Bible] all day than rinse my hand in several chapters."

———

Do not let this Book of the Law depart from your mouth; meditate on it day and night.

JOSHUA 1:8 NIV

LOST IN HIS VASTNESS

"As well might a gnat seek to drink in the ocean, as a finite creature to comprehend the Eternal God."

When I consider thy heavens, the work of thy fingers, the moon and the stars, which thou hast ordained; what is man that thou art mindful of him?

PSALM 8:3-4

DID YOU KNOW?

He did not like the term "Reverend" because it was not biblical and smacked of pride. He intentionally was not ordained as a Baptist minister, but accepted the title of "Pastor."

HE SHOULDERS THE BURDEN

"The heaviest end of the cross lies ever on His shoulders. If He bids us carry a burden, He carries it also."

———

Take my yoke upon you and learn from me, for I am gentle and humble in heart, and you will find rest for your souls.

MATTHEW 11:29 NIV

A RESERVOIR OF LOVE

"The heart of Christ became like a reservoir... All the...streams of iniquity, and every drop of the sins of His people, ran down and gathered into one vast lake, deep as hell and shoreless as eternity. All these met...in Christ's heart and He endured them all."

You will again have compassion on us; you will tread our sins underfoot and hurl all our iniquities into the depths of the sea.

MICAH 7:19 NIV

HELL-SHATTERING NEWS

"The preaching of Christ is the whip that flogs the devil...the thunderbolt... which makes all hell shake."

Thou believest that there is one God; thou doest well: the devils also believe, and tremble.

JAMES 2:19

DID YOU KNOW?

He denounced American slavery, saying the Civil War was
necessary if it meant abolition.

KEEN-EYED ENVY

"Nothing sharpens sight like envy. It spies out the smallest fault, but at the same time refuses to see anything which might excuse it."

———————

But if ye have bitter envying and strife in your hearts, glory not, and lie not against the truth.

JAMES 3:14

FILTHY RICH

"Riches, like manure, do not do good till they are spread...Fork them out. Dispurse and disperse. What heaps now lie reeking up offensively to heaven!"

Sell your possessions and give to the poor. Provide purses for yourselves that will not wear out, a treasure in heaven that will not be exhausted.

LUKE 12:33 NIV

GIVE IN AND WIN

"Stoop to conquer. He who yields wins. It is so in the Christian life. We are to be anvils, and overcome the hammers, not by striking again, but by patiently bearing the blows."

If someone strikes you on one cheek, turn to him the other also.

LUKE 6:29 NIV

DID YOU KNOW?

Spurgeon was exposed to illness, slander, depression, and tragedy. In the latter case, false cries of "Fire" in a church service killed seven.

NO MEETING HALFWAY

"Halfway to Christ is a dreadful place; for it tempts to presumption, and yet it is no better than being far off."

So then because thou art lukewarm, and neither cold nor hot, I will spue thee out of my mouth.

REVELATION 3:16

MANAGE FEW THINGS WELL

"If you meddle with many things, you will muddle them all. Some few seem to be able to manage many things; but, as a rule, if we have too many irons in the fire, some of them burn."

And let the peace of God rule in your hearts.

COLOSSIANS 3:15

HIDING PURPOSES, NOT PROMISES

"God conceals His purposes, that we may live on His promises. It is not for us to pry into His decrees or seek to know the future; the promise should be sufficient to stay the heart as to the Lord's ways."

Surely I spoke of things I did not understand, things too wonderful for me to know.

JOB 42:3 NIV

A WELL-STRUNG BOW

"Praying without working is a bow without string.... If the man desired that which he pretends to pray for, he would be eager to labor for it."

But be ye doers of the word, and not hearers only, deceiving your own selves.

JAMES 1:22

A RABBI'S ADVICE

"Pay thy tithe, and be rich.
So say the Rabbis. Nothing is gained
by robbing God."

_____

*And of all thou shalt give me I will
surely give the tenth unto thee.*

GENESIS 28:22

MUCH MORE THAN BIRDS

"God, who feeds His ravens, will feed His doves. Or, as Matthew Henry puts it, 'He that feeds his birds will not starve his babes.'"

Behold the fowls of the air: For they sow not, neither do they reap, nor gather into barns; yet your heavenly Father feedeth them. Are ye not much better than they?

MATTHEW 6:26

DID YOU KNOW?

There have been more books imprinted by Charles Haddon Spurgeon in the last hundred years than by any other Christian author, living or dead. He is history's most widely read preacher. At least three of his books have sold over a million copies.

CHARIOTS OF FIRE

"God's chariots of fire conquer men's chariots of iron. He has forces of a spiritual order which prevail over the most stubborn wills and the strongest arms."

For sin shall not have dominion over you: for ye are not under the law, but under grace.

ROMANS 6:14

TRY, TRY AGAIN

"Nothing endeavored, nothing discovered. If we do not try we shall never find out the way. Without effort we shall stick in the mud, and never get further."

Ask, and it shall be given you; seek, and ye shall find; knock and it shall be opened unto you.

MATTHEW 7:7

CROSS BEFORE CROWN

"Jesus has many lovers of His crown, but few bearers of His cross."

If any man will come after me, let him deny himself, and take up his cross, and follow me.

MATTHEW 16:24

DID YOU KNOW?

Spurgeon's only children, twin sons, Thomas and Charles, Jr., both became preachers like their illustrious father.

IRON NOW, GOLD LATER

"Look not for a golden life in an iron world. Where Jesus wore a crown of thorns we cannot expect coronets of honor."

Now if we are children, then we are heirs — heirs of God and co-heirs with Christ, if indeed we share in his sufferings in order that we may also share in his glory.

ROMANS 8:17 NIV

A "PRIME" MINISTER

"Spurgeon was the greatest preacher of his age...I never heard anything like it."

—words of Prime Minister David Lloyd George

OUR NEW DEFENSE LAWYER

[An old ploughman said], "The other day, sir, the devil was tempting me and I tried to answer him; but I found he was an old lawyer, and understood the law a great deal better than I did, so I gave over, and would not argue with him anymore; so I said to him, 'What do you trouble me for?'" "'Why,' said he, 'about your soul.'"

"'Oh!' said I, 'that is no business of mine; I have given my soul over into the hand of Christ; I have transferred everything to Him; if you want an answer to your doubts and queries, you must apply to my Advocate.'"

And if any man sin, we have an advocate with the Father, Jesus Christ the righteous.

1 JOHN 2:1

DID YOU KNOW?

His most profound book may have been *The Treasury of David*, a massive commentary on the Psalms which took over twenty years to research.

"The Lord gets His best soldiers out of the highlands of affliction."

HIGHLAND SOLDIERS

Blessed is the man that endureth temptation: for when he is tried, he shall receive the crown of life, which the Lord hath promised to them that love him.

JAMES 1:12

SETTING OUR SOULS ALOFT

"We must see to it that we are uplifted as near to God as possible. All our power will depend upon the elevation of our spirits. Prayer, meditation, devotion, communion, are like a windlass to wind us up aloft."

***

Come near to God and he will come near to you.

JAMES 4:8 NIV

HIS GLORY OUR AIM

"He who makes God's glory the one and only aim before which all other things bow themselves, is the man to bring honor to his Lord."

Give unto the Lord the glory due unto his name.

PSALM 29:2

AN IMPORTANT WORD

"Learn to say no; it will be of more use to you than to be able to read."

Whoso keepeth his mouth and his tongue keepeth his soul from troubles.

PROVERBS 21:23

NEEDY MORNING AND NIGHT

"We never wake up in the morning but we want strength for the day, and we never go to bed at night without needing grace to cover the sins of the past."

Give us today our daily bread. Forgive us our debts.

MATTHEW 6:11-12 NIV

SERVE ONE OR THE OTHER

"All attempts to serve God and to serve the world too must end in bitter failure."

No servant can serve two masters.
LUKE 16:13

A GALAXY OF SPLENDOR

"When you contemplate the Savior, you find all the virtues enshrined in Him; other men are stars, but He is a constellation, nay, He is the whole universe of stars gathered into one galaxy of splendor; other men are gems and jewels, but He is the crown imperial, where every jewel glitters."

Be thou exalted, O God, above the heavens: and thy glory above all the earth.

PSALM 108:5

GRAND BUT DIFFICULT

"Many men owe the grandeur of their lives to their tremendous difficulties."

When you walk through the fire, you will not be burned; the flames will not set you ablaze. For I am the Lord your God.

ISAIAH 43:2-3 NIV

DID YOU KNOW?

He helped start Stockwell orphanage and
Pastor's College. Over 900 students were
educated at the college during his lifetime.

IF THE SHOE PINCHES

"Go with your neighbor as far as good conscience will go with you, but part company where the shoe of conscience begins to pinch your foot."

Blessed is the man who does not walk in the counsel of the wicked or stand in the way of sinners or sit in the seat of mockers.

PSALM 1:1

THE BRIGHTER SIDE

"If one door shall be shut, God will open another; if the peas do not yield well, the beans may; if one hen leaves her eggs, another will bring all her brood; there's a bright side to all things, and a good God everywhere."

And we know that all things work together for good to them that love God.

ROMANS 8:28

TRUST AND OBEY

"Faith and obedience are bound up in the same bundle; he that obeys God trusts God; and he that trusts God obeys God."

If a man love me, he will keep my words: and my Father will love him, and we will come unto him, and make our abode with him.

JOHN 14:23

DID YOU KNOW?

One Saturday night he preached a sermon in his sleep. His wife gave him a detailed summary the next morning. A few hours later he preached that sermon to his congregation!

HIS RELIANCE ON PRAYER

"Let me have your prayers, and I can do anything! Let me be without my people's prayers, and I can do nothing!"

For the eyes of the Lord are over the righteous, and his ears are open unto their prayers.

1 PETER 3:12

HEARTS IN PUBLIC VIEW

"With heaven there are no secrets. That which is done in the private chamber of the heart is as public as the streets before the all-seeing eye."

Shall not God search this out? For he knoweth the secrets of the heart.

PSALM 44:21

DON'T EXPECT MUCH

"If we would always recollect that we live among men who are imperfect, we should not be in such a fever when we find out our friend's failings; what's rotten will rend, and cracked pots will leak."

Why do you look at the speck of sawdust in your brother's eye and pay no attention to the plank in your own eye?

LUKE 6:41 NIV

SWEET FRIEND

"Friendship is one of the sweetest joys of life. Many might have failed beneath the bitterness of their trial had they not found a friend."

_____

A friend loveth at all times.

PROVERBS 17:17

HE LOVES US ANYWAY

"With all our faults God loves us still, if we are trusting in His Son, therefore let us not be downhearted, but hope to live and learn, and do some good service before we die."

My goodness, and my fortress; my high tower, and my deliverer; my shield, and he in whom I trust.

PSALM 144:2

"GOODS" IN STORAGE

"To keep the chaff out of a bushel, one sure plan is to fill it full of wheat; and to keep out vain thoughts, it is wise and prudent to have the mind stored with choice subjects for meditation."

Whatsoever things are true, whatsoever things are honest, whatsoever things are just, whatsoever things are pure, whatsoever things are lovely, whatsoever things are of good report; if there be any virtue, and if there be any praise, think on these things.

PHILIPPIANS 4:8

KNOWLEDGE OR IGNORANCE?

"The doorstep to the temple of wisdom is the knowledge of our own ignorance."

———

With the lowly is wisdom.

PROVERBS 11:2

BALANCING YOUR SECRETS

"Commit all your secrets to no man; trust in God with all your heart, but let your confidence in friends be weighed in balances of prudence."

Trust in the Lord with all your heart and lean not on your own understanding; in all your ways acknowledge him, and he will make your paths straight.

PROVERBS 3:5-6 NIV

DID YOU KNOW?

During nearly four decades of ministry he added
14,000 new members to his church alone.

A PAPER BOAT TO HEAVEN

"One might better try to sail the Atlantic in a paper boat than to get to heaven in good works."

For by grace are ye saved through faith; and that not of yourselves: it is the gift of God.

EPHESIANS 2:8

LUCK REQUIRES WORK

"Luck generally comes to those who look after it, and my notion is that it taps at least once in a lifetime at everybody's door, but if industry does not open it, away it goes."

If any would not work, neither should he eat.

2 THESSALONIANS 3:10

ANCHORED IN THE BOOK

"A man ought to hope within the bounds of reason and the promises of the good old Book. Hope leans on an anchor, but an anchor must have something to hold by and to hold to."

Happy is he that hath the God of Jacob for his help, whose hope is in the Lord his God.

PSALM 146:5

SINKING IN THE MUD

"A man pays Peter with what he has borrowed of Paul, and thinks he is getting out of his difficulties, when he is putting one foot in the mud to pull his other foot out."

The rich ruleth over the poor, and the borrower is servant to the lender.

PROVERBS 22:7

FOOLS WHO KNOW MUCH

"There is no fool so great a fool as a knowing fool. But to know how to use knowledge is to have wisdom."

The way of a fool is right in his own eyes: but he that hearkeneth unto counsel is wise.

PROVERBS 12:15

THE CHURCH IN YOUR HOUSE

"Our house ought to be a little church, with holiness to the Lord over the door, but it ought never to be a prison where there is plenty of rule and order, but little love and no pleasure."

But as for me and my house, we will serve the Lord.

JOSHUA 24:15

BOUND BUT NOT CRUSHED

"The husband should be the house-band, binding all together like a cornerstone, but not crushing everything like a millstone."

_____

Husbands, love your wives, and be not bitter against them.

COLOSSIANS 3:19

THE BETTER HALF OF LIFE

"A true wife is her husband's better half, his lump of delight, his flower of beauty, his guardian angel, and his heart's treasure."

Who can find a virtuous woman? For her price is far above rubies.

PROVERBS 31:10

GREASE THAT PRODUCES GOLD

"Hard work is the grand secret of success. Nothing but rags and poverty can come of idleness. Elbow grease is the only stuff to make gold with."

And whatsoever ye do, do it heartily, as to the Lord, and not unto men.

COLOSSIANS 3:23

HEAR NO EVIL

"You cannot stop people's tongues, and therefore the best thing to do is to stop your own ears and never mind what is spoken."

But no man can tame the tongue. It is a restless evil full of deadly poison.

JAMES 3:8 NIV

A SLUGGISH HEART

"The Lord Jesus tells us Himself that when men slept, the enemy sowed the tares; and that hits the nail on the head, for it is by the door of sluggishness that evil enters the heart, more often, it seems to me, than by any other."

A little sleep, a little slumber, a little folding of the hands to rest — and poverty will come on you like a bandit and scarcity like an armed man.

Proverbs 6:10-11

87

DID YOU KNOW?

He read *The Pilgrim's Progress* over 100 times, starting at age six. He never attended college, but read over six books a week and could remember what he read years later. He had over 12,000 volumes in his library.

THORNS, NOT GRAPES

"A man might as well hope, as our Lord says, to gather grapes of thorns, or figs of thistles, as look for a happy hereafter at the end of a bad life."

Do not be deceived: God cannot be mocked. A man reaps what he sows.

GALATIANS 6:7 NIV

HELP FOR THE HELPLESS

"God helps those who cannot help themselves."

God is our refuge and strength, a very present help in trouble.

PSALM 46:1

DEATH BREATHES LIFE

"Nothing puts life into men like a dying Savior."

O death, where is thy sting? O grave, where is thy victory?

1 Corinthians 15:55

THE POWER OF A SENTENCE

"I hold one single sentence out of God's Word to be of more certainty and of more power than all the discoveries of all the learned men of all the ages."

I will bow down toward your holy temple and will praise your name for your love and your faithfulness, for you have exalted above all things your name and your word.

PSALM 138:2 NIV

A MISSION OF TRUTH

"Every Christian is either a missionary or an impostor."

Go ye therefore, and teach all nations, baptizing them in the name of the Father, and of the Son, and of the Holy Ghost.

MATTHEW 28:19

WE NAILED HIM TO A CROSS

"Sin is Christicide."

God made him who had no sin to be sin for us, so that in him we might become the righteousness of God.

2 CORINTHIANS 5:21 NIV

DID YOU KNOW?

One woman became converted from a single page of his sermon wrapped around some butter. A worker high in the church rafter accepted Christ as Spurgeon tested the acoustics with a single Gospel sentence.

PRAY ALWAYS

"I always feel that there is something wrong if I go without prayer for even [a] half an hour in the day."

Pray without ceasing.
1 THESSALONIANS 5:17

THE FAMILY FOUNDATION

"I am sure we cannot expect our children to grow up a godly seed if there is no family prayer."

Do not forget the things your eyes have seen or let them slip from your heart as long as you live. Teach them to your children and to their children after them.

DEUTERONOMY 4:9 NIV

A LIE SPOILS EVERYTHING

"I would not utter what I believed to be a falsehood concerning the Lord, even though the evil one offered me the bait of saving all mankind thereby."

Therefore each of you must put off falsehood and speak truthfully to his neighbor, for we are all members of one body.

EPHESIANS 4:25 NIV

GOD'S GREATEST MIRACLE

"The greatest of all miracles is the salvation of a soul."

———————

For God so loved the world, that he gave his only begotten Son, that whosoever believeth in him should not perish, but have everlasting life.

JOHN 3:16

BACK-SLIDING STANDING STILL

"If you want to know how to backslide, leave off going forward. Cease going upward and you will go downward of necessity. You can never stand still."

As newborn babes, desire the sincere milk of the word, that ye may grow thereby.

1 PETER 2:2

DID YOU KNOW?

Men would be interested to know that his wife Susannah called him "Tinshatha," which means "Your Excellency."

WORLDLINESS AND GOD'S WORD

"Worldliness has gone a long way to destroy the Church of God. I judge it to be the worst cankerworm that assails us."

For the wisdom of this world is foolishness in God's sight.

1 CORINTHIANS 3:19 NIV

LOVE IS TAX FREE

"In the religion of Christ there is not taxation. Everything is of love."

Each man should give what he has decided in his heart to give, not reluctantly or under compulsion, for God loves a cheerful giver.

2 CORINTHIANS 9:7 NIV

THE TRIALS OF HIS SON

"God had one Son without sin, but He never had a Son without trial."

Then he said to them, "My soul is overwhelmed with sorrow to the point of death."

MATTHEW 26:38 NIV

FIVE MINUTES OF BLISS

"I would sooner possess the joy of Christ five minutes than I would revel in the mirth of fools for half a century."

The hope of the righteous shall be gladness.

PROVERBS 10:28

THE JOY OF SERVICE

"I think I know of no delight on earth that is higher than that of knowing that you really are with all your heart adoringly serving God."

What does the Lord your God ask of you but to fear the Lord your God, to walk in all his ways, to love him, to serve the Lord your God with all your heart and with all your soul.

DEUTERONOMY 10:12 NIV

EVERYTHING IS GOLDEN

"You cannot buy heaven with gold. Why, they pave the streets up there with it."

"Come!" Whoever is thirsty ...let him take the free gift of the water of life.

REVELATION 22:17 NIV

HAVE IT GOD'S WAY

"When your will is God's will, you will have your will."

But seek ye first the kingdom of God, and his righteousness; and all these things shall be added unto you.

MATTHEW 6:33

EARTHLY WARFARE

"It strikes me that conflict is the principal feature of the Christian life this side of heaven."

In the world ye shall have tribulation: but be of good cheer; I have overcome the world.

JOHN 16:33

*DOUBLE
IS STILL
NOTHING*

"If you are not content with what you
have, you would not be satisfied
if it were doubled."

_I have learned, in whatsoever state
I am, therewith to be content._

PHILIPPIANS 4:11

"Be walking Bibles."

LIVE THE BOOK

Impress [these commandments] on your children. Talk about them when you sit at home and when you walk along the road, when you lie down and when you get up.

DEUTERONOMY 6:7 NIV

LOSING IT FOR GOOD

"When I hear of anybody losing his temper, I always pray that he may not find it again. Such tempers are best lost."

A fool gives full vent to his anger, but a wise man keeps himself under control.

PROVERBS 29:11 NIV

DID YOU KNOW?

His local congregation numbered over 5,000 and he once spoke to an audience of over 23,000 without any amplification. It is estimated that he preached to over ten million people!

THE SPRING-TIME OF MY SOUL

"Lord, end my winter, and let my spring begin. I cannot with all my longing raise my soul out of her death and dullness, but all things are possible with Thee. I need celestial influences, the clear shinings of Thy love, the beams of Thy grace, the light of Thy countenance."

Create in me a clean heart, O God; and renew a right spirit within me.

PSALM 51:10

A GARDEN WATERED WITH TEARS

"To continue still to mourn sin is to continue to grow in grace. Tear drops are blessed watering for the flowers of grace."

He giveth grace unto the lowly.
PROVERBS 3:34

WHAT DO YOU WITHHOLD?

"Our gifts are not to be measured by the amount we contribute, but by the surplus kept in our own hand."

———

See that you also excel in thIS grace of giving.

2 CORINTHIANS 8:7 NIV

HIS DARKEST HOURS

"I often feel very grateful to God that I have undergone fearful depression. I know the borders of despair and the horrible brink of that gulf of darkness into which my feet have almost gone. But hundreds of times I have been able to give a helpful grip to brethren and sisters who have come into the same condition."

"I believe that the darkest and most dreadful experience of a child of God will help him to be a fisher of men if he will but follow Christ."

If we are distressed, it is for your comfort and salvation; if we are comforted, it is for your comfort, which produces in you patient endurance of the same sufferings we suffer.

2 CORINTHIANS 1:6 NIV

SLEEPING IN CHURCH

"I believe a very large majority of churchgoers are merely unthinking, slumbering worshipers of an unknown God."

His watchmen are blind; they are all ignorant, they are all dumb dogs, they cannot bark; sleeping, lying down, loving to slumber.

ISAIAH 56:10

A WIFE'S COMMITMENT

"It was ever the settled purpose of my married life that I should never hinder him in his work for the Lord, never try to keep him from fulfilling his engagements, never plead my own ill-health as a reason why he should remain at home with me." (Susannah Spurgeon)

A woman that feareth the Lord, she shall be praised.

PROVERBS 31:30

A SOFTER VERSION OF GOD

"The glory of the divine Trinity overawes us until we behold the milder radiance of the Incarnate God."

_____

You will find a baby wrapped in cloths and lying in a manger.

LUKE 2:12 NIV

THE WINE OF AFFLICTION

"Rutherford had a quaint saying, that when he was cast into the cellars of affliction, he remembered that the great King always kept His wine there."

But he lifted the needy out of their affliction and increased their families like flocks.

PSALM 107:41 NIV

FOLLOWING THROUGH CONSISTENTLY

"We judge of a man's zeal when the purpose has been long in his heart, and he has most industriously followed it through a long period."

———

Let us run with patience the race that is set before us.

HEBREWS 12:1

MY LORD, MY EVERYTHING

"What is it to believe in Him? It is not merely to say, "He is God and the Savior," but to trust Him wholly and entirely, and take Him for all your salvation from this time forth and forever—your Lord, your Master, your All."

The Lord is high above all nations, and his glory above the heavens.

PSALM 113:4

DID YOU KNOW?

His printed sermons contained sixty-three volumes
and are the largest set of books by a single
author in the history of Christianity.

THE CLEAR LIGHT OF SCRIPTURE

"Scripture is...a rock of diamonds; it is a sacred collyrium, or eye-salve; it mends their eyes that look upon it; it is a spiritual optic-glass in which the glory of God is resplendent."

_____

But his delight is in the law of the Lord; and in his law doth he meditate day and night.

PSALM 1:2

FEAST ON HIS JOYFUL PRESENCE

"Christ being present with you, this is your main joy. Enjoy the feast for yourselves, or you will not be strong to hand out the living bread to others."

———————

I am the bread of life: he that cometh to me shall never hunger; and he that believeth on me shall never thirst.

JOHN 6:35

"Holy wonder will lead you to
grateful worship."

WONDERFUL WORSHIP

*How awesome is the Lord
Most High, the great King
over all the earth!*

PSALM 47:2 NIV NIV

"Virtues without faith are whitewashed sins. Unbelief nullifies everything."

HOLLOW VIRTUES

And without faith it is impossible to please God, because anyone who comes to him must believe that he exists and that he rewards those who earnestly seek him.

HEBREWS 11:6 NIV

HOLD FAST FOR TRUTH

"Yield in all things personal, but be firm where truth and holiness are concerned."

And we are his house, if we hold on to our courage and the hope of which we boast.

HEBREWS 3:6 NIV

WASHED ON THE RIGHT SHORE

"The law is a storm which wrecks your hopes of self-salvation, but washes you upon the Rock of Ages."

God [sent] his own Son in the likeness of sinful flesh, and for sin, condemned sin in the flesh: that the righteousness of the law might be fulfilled in us, who walk not after the flesh, but after the Spirit.

ROMANS 8:3-4

THE GOSPEL'S CONTINUING POWER

"Still the gospel breaks, and still it makes whole; still it wounds, and still it quickens; still it seems to hurl men down to hell in their terrible experience of the evil of sin, but still it lifts them up into an ecstatic joy, till they are exalted almost to heaven when they lay hold upon it, and feel its power in their souls."

For I am not ashamed of the gospel of Christ; for it is the power of God unto salvation to every one that believeth.

ROMANS 1:16

A TASTE OF ETERNAL COMMUNION

"The Holy Spirit is not only the pledge but the foretaste of everlasting bliss...His influence over us brings us that same communion with God which we shall enjoy for ever in Heaven."

And hereby we know that he abideth in us, by the Spirit which he hath given us.

1 JOHN 3:24

STANDING ON THE PROMISES

"We are persuaded to try the trembling legs of our faith by the sight of a promise."

But in keeping with his promise we are looking forward to a new heaven and a new earth, the home of righteousness.

2 PETER 3:13 NIV

SOLID GROUND

"Faith without promise would be a foot without ground to stand upon."

_____

Faith is the substance of things hoped for, the evidence of things not seen.

HEBREWS 11:1

FAITH HAS MORE ROOM

"Many a believer lives in the cottage of doubt when he might live in the mansion of faith."

———

But when he asks, he must believe and not doubt, because he who doubts is like a wave on the sea, blown and tossed by the wind.

JAMES 1:6 NIV

FIRED UP FOR GOD

"Your sermons—make them red hot; never mind if men say you are too enthusiastic or even too fanatical."

Now we exhort you, brethren, warn them that are unruly, comfort the feebleminded, support the weak, be patient toward all men.

1 THESSALONIANS 5:14

DID YOU KNOW?

Like Wesley, he came from a line of ministers. Both his
father John and his grandfather James shepherded
independent evangelical churches.

BRIDGE OVER TROUBLED WATER

"Bridge there is none: we must go through the waters, and feel the rush of the rivers. The presence of God in the flood is better than a ferry boat. Tried we must be, but triumphant we shall be; for Jehovah Himself, who is mightier than many waters, shall be with us."

The Lord upholdeth all that fall, and raiseth up all those that be bowed down.

PSALM 145:14

FAITH IN DIFFICULTY

"Faith about my pain, my poverty, my despondency, my old age— that is faith."

Commit thy way unto the Lord; trust also in him; and he shall bring it to pass.

PSALM 37:5

PLEASE JOIN ME

"Mention your own experience—and plead with men to come and taste the same."

And they said, Believe on the Lord Jesus Christ, and thou shalt be saved, and thy house.

Acts 16:31

PROMISES ARE A WEAPON

"You will handle faith well if you are able to quote the promises of God against the attacks of your enemy."

Let you conversation be always full of grace, seasoned with salt, so that you may know how to answer everyone.

COLOSSIANS 4:6 NIV

"Lord, make me watchful in little matters, lest I grow careless in weightier concerns."

AVOID SMALL ERRORS

Whoever can be trusted with very little can also be trusted with much, and whoever is dishonest with very little will also be dishonest with much.

LUKE 16:10 NIV

DRESS REHEARSAL

"Praise is the rehearsal of our eternal song. By grace we learn to sing, and in glory we continue to sing."

Sing unto God, ye kingdoms of the earth; O sing praises unto the Lord.

PSALM 68:32

A PEARL OF GREAT PRICE

"Patience is a pearl which is only found in the deep seas of affliction; and only grace can find it there, bring it to the surface, and adorn the neck of faith therewith."

I waited patiently for the Lord; and he inclined unto me, and heard my cry.

PSALM 40:1

DEEP, NOT LONG

"Some brethren pray by the yard; but true prayer is measured by weight, and not by length."

————————

The Lord...he heareth the prayer of the righteous.

PROVERBS 15:29

A REWARDING JOURNEY

"From prayer to praise is never a long or difficult journey."

———

He shall pray unto God, and he will be favorable unto him: and he shall see his face with joy: for he will render unto man his righteousness.

JOB 33:26

DID YOU KNOW?

Spurgeon had friends in Hudson Taylor and George Mueller. His secular associations included Prime Minister Gladstone and art historian John Ruskin.

THE BOOK'S PROTECTION

"A true love for the great Book will bring us great peace from the great God, and be a great protection to us."

For everything that was written in the past was written to teach us, so that through endurance and the encouragement of the Scriptures we might have hope.

ROMANS 15:4 NIV

THE MEDICINE OF GRACE

"Grace is the best of restoratives; divine love is the safest stimulant for a languishing patient; it makes the soul strong as a giant, even when the bones are breaking through the skin."

For you have been born again, not of perishable seed, but of imperishable, through the living and enduring word of God.

1 PETER 1:23 NIV

HAD FOR THE SEEKING

"We need our God; He is to be had for the seeking; and He will not deny Himself to any one of us if we personally seek His face."

Call unto me, and I will answer thee, and shew thee great and mighty things, which thou knowest not.

JEREMIAH 33:3

A JUDGE OF THE GOOD

"Many pleasing things the Lord may withhold, but 'no good thing.' He is the best judge of what is good for us."

Every good gift and every perfect gift is from above.

JAMES 1:17

DID YOU KNOW?

Like Moody, he appealed to the common working person. He often used word pictures and spoke simply to their deepest needs. He paced the platform and took on dramatic roles of Bible characters to communicate the gospel.

AN EAR FOR CHRIST

"We must hear Jesus speak if we expect Him to hear us speak. If we have no ear for Christ, He will have no ear for us."

Thou shalt guide me with thy counsel.

PSALM 73: 24

SPECIAL STRENGTH

"Do we not remember seasons of labor and trial in which we received such special strength that we wondered at ourselves? God gives unexpected strength when unusual trials come upon us."

I will not leave you comfortless: I will come to you.

JOHN 14:18

STANDING ON THE SERPENT

"Shortly we shall set our foot on the old serpent! What a joy to crush evil! What dishonor to Satan to have his head bruised by human feet! Let us by faith in Jesus tread the tempter down."

Submit yourselves therefore to God. Resist the devil, and he will flee from you.

JAMES 4:7

REVERENCE TIED TO JOY

"Unless we do have deep awe of the Word we shall never have high joy over it. Our rejoicing will be measured by our reverencing."

―――――――

To him be glory and dominion for ever and ever. Amen.

1 PETER 5:11

GOODNESS WITH ALL YOUR HEART

"Be dogmatically true, obstinately holy, immovably honest, desperately kind, fixedly upright."

He that followeth after righteous-ness and mercy findeth life, righteousness, and honour.

PROVERBS 21:21

DID YOU KNOW?

Over 60,000 attended the funeral procession. His deathbed words were: "My work is done. I have fought the good fight. I have finished my course. I have kept the faith."

Additional copies of this book
and other titles from **Honor Books**
are available at your local bookstore:

D.L. Moody's Little Instruction Book
John Wesley's Little Instruction Book
Larry Burkett's Little Instruction Book
Martin Luther's Little Instruction Book
Tozer's Little Instruction Book
God's Little Instruction Book (series)
God's Little Devotional Book (series)

Tulsa, Oklahoma